CONTENTS

Some words are shown in bold, **like this**. You can find out what they mean by looking in the glossary.

WHAT IS JUDAISM?

There are over 13 million followers of Judaism, the Jewish religion. Jews believe that there is only one God. They follow the Ten Commandments and other rules of life, which they believe come from God. Jews gather to pray and learn in **synagogues,** which are Jewish places of worship. Jewish religious teachers and leaders are called rabbis.

≫ The main types of Judaism in the United Kingdom are called Orthodox, Reform and Liberal.

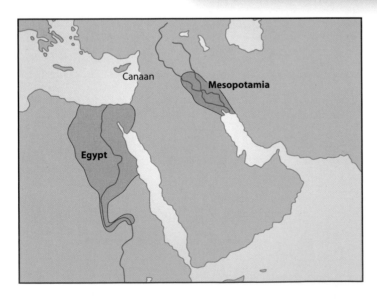

Canaan

Mesopotamia

Egypt

≪ This is a map of the Middle East at around the time when the Jewish religion began. For example, Egypt's borders are very different today.

Abraham and Moses

The Jewish religion began over 3,000 years ago in the Middle East. It is written in the **Hebrew Bible** that God told a man called Abraham to move from his home in Mesopotamia (now Iraq) to Canaan (Palestine). God said that if he obeyed, Abraham, his children and their children would become a great nation. The agreement between Abraham and God is called a **covenant**. Later, the people became known as **Israelites**.

The Israelites later became **slaves** in Egypt. A man called Moses led them to freedom, back to Canaan. The Jews believe that God divided the sea so that they could pass safely. The sea then closed again, drowning the Egyptian army who were chasing them. This event is called the Exodus.

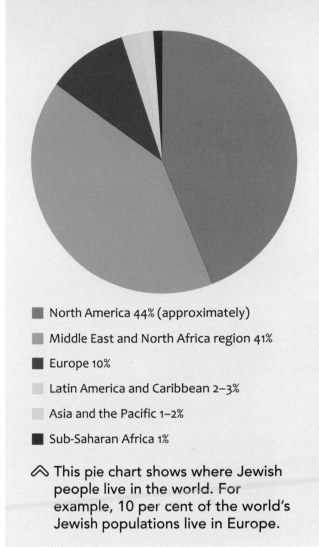

■ North America 44% (approximately)

■ Middle East and North Africa region 41%

■ Europe 10%

Latin America and Caribbean 2–3%

Asia and the Pacific 1–2%

■ Sub-Saharan Africa 1%

⌃ This pie chart shows where Jewish people live in the world. For example, 10 per cent of the world's Jewish populations live in Europe.

God gave Moses many commandments to follow, of which the "Ten Commandments" are the most famous. God would look after the Israelites if they followed these commands.

Holy Books

The **Torah** (the first five books of the holy Hebrew Bible) is believed to have been given by God to Moses on Mount Sinai. Torah means "teaching and law". It is the most holy of Jewish books and includes the Ten Commandments. The Talmud is an important record of discussions on the meaning of the Torah.

Festivals

Many important dates in the Jewish calendar are a time of celebration and eating special foods. For example, sweet dishes made from cheese, such as cheesecake, are eaten at Shavuot, which celebrates the time when God gave the Torah to Moses.

As well as fun celebrations, there are more serious days. Yom Kippur, the Day of Atonement, is when people ask God for forgiveness for their sins.

The Holocaust

The International **Holocaust** Remembrance Day is on both Jewish and non-Jewish calendars throughout the world. It commemorates the millions murdered by the Nazis, including 6 million Jews, during **World War II**.

⌃ The Memorial to the Murdered Jews of Europe (also called the Holocaust Memorial) in Berlin, Germany.

A day of rest

Shabbat (the Hebrew for Sabbath) is a weekly holy day. It begins every Friday night and ends at nightfall on Saturday. It is a day of rest, when Jews stop work so that they can go to the synagogue, and give more time to God.

⩟ Shabbat begins with the family sharing a meal.

The Jewish calendar

Jewish celebrations are the same date each year on the Jewish calendar. However, on the Gregorian calendar (the calendar most often used in countries like the UK), they fall on different dates. This is because the Jewish calendar follows the Moon's cycle, while the Gregorian calendar follows the Sun's cycle.

The Jewish calendar has 11 fewer days every year, but a month is added every two or three years to make up for this. The Jewish day begins at sunset, so all the celebrations or festivals begin the evening before their date on the Gregorian calendar.

JEWISH CALENDAR

The dates of the festivals are approximate and change each year:

1. Nisan (March/April) – 5 Purim, 15–22 Pesach, 27 **Holocaust** Memorial Day
2. Iyyar (falls between April and June)
3. Sivan (May/June) – 6 Shavuot
4. Tammuz (June/July)
5. Av (July/August)
6. Elul (August/September)
7. Tishri (September/October) – 1–2 Rosh Hashanah (New Year), 10 Yom Kippur (Day of Atonement), 15–21 Sukkot
8. Heshvan (or Chesvan) (October/November)
9. Kislev (November/December) – 25 1st day of Hannukah
10. Tevet (December/January) – 2 last day of Hannukah
11. Shevat (January/Feburary)
12. Adar (Adar II on a leap year, falls between February and March) 14 Purim

Rosh Hashanah

Rosh Hashanah means the "head of the year" and is the Jewish New Year festival. It lasts for two days.

Unlike many modern New Year celebrations, Rosh Hashanah does not involve parties. It is a time when Jews think quietly about their own values and behaviour. The festival is also known as the Day of Judgement, the Day of the Sounding of the Shofar and the Day of Remembrance.

Why is it so important?

The festival is important for two main reasons:

- It is a time to think about the creation of the world, the time when it is believed that God made the first humans, Adam and Eve.

- It marks the beginning of the Days of Awe or **Repentance** – 10 days in which Jews must think about the way they have behaved in the last year. They ask God for forgiveness and are also expected to apologize to people they have upset. Jewish people work out how they can behave better in the year ahead.

The sounding of the shofar

Rosh Hashanah is a holiday, and a lot of time is spent in the synagogue for special prayers. A hundred notes are blown on the shofar (an instrument made from a ram's horn) each day, unless Rosh Hashanah falls on a Shabbat. It is thought to be a wake-up call to repent.

≫ A rabbi blowing a shofar.

Sweet New Year

After the service on the first day, a special meal is eaten at home. Eating sweet foods such as honey cake, or lekach, and apple dipped in honey is a way of wishing everyone a sweet (happy) New Year.

Kosher

Jews have to follow certain laws about food. Foods that fit in with the laws are called kosher. Some foods, for example pork, are forbidden. Birds and mammals have to be killed and prepared in a certain way for meat. Meat cannot be eaten in the same meal as dairy products, such as milk, butter and eggs.

⌃ Sweet foods, such as honey and fruit, are eaten at Rosh Hashanah. Rosh Hashanah means "head of the year", so a fish head is eaten.

The Day of Atonement

Yom Kippur is a very important day for Jews. It is known as the Day of Atonement because on this day Jews atone (make amends) with God, asking for God's forgiveness for any wrongdoings. Yom Kippur is everyone's last chance to gain forgiveness before God's judgement is finalized. It is the end of a 10-day cycle that began with Rosh Hashanah.

Jews do not go to work on Yom Kippur – they pray and **fast** for 25 hours. Most of the day is spent in the synagogue. The last service ends with a blast of the shofar.

The final meal

Before sunset, when the fast begins, everyone has a final meal called the seudah ha-mafseket. The meal is usually soup and chicken. Prayers are said over wine and **challah**, the traditional Jewish bread.

⌃ Jews gather to say their Yom Kippur prayers at the Western Wall, the only remaining part of the Jerusalem temple that was destroyed by the Romans in 70 CE.

Different groups

There are various Jewish movements in the United Kingdom and the United States. Orthodox and ultra-Orthodox Jews are more traditional and strict in their observance of **Jewish Law**. Other groups are more flexible.

Jewish communities come from different areas, too. The Ashkenazi come from Germany and traditionally speak a blend of German and **Hebrew** called Yiddish. The Sephardi are descended from Spanish Jews and speak Ladino. Different groups celebrate festivals in different ways. They may have different foods, or festivals which are observed over a different number of days.

⌄ North London's Orthodox Jewish community is the biggest in Europe and they strictly follow Jewish Law. For example, they don't let men and women mix at public events.

Honey
cake

Happy New Year! At Rosh Hashanah, Jewish families often eat lekach, or honey cake. This sweet cake – with honey, sugar and raisins – is a way to welcome the hopeful sweetness of a new year.

TIME:

About 1 hour

SERVES:

8 people (2 squares each)

TOOLS:

mixing bowls
weighing scales
spatula
electric hand mixer
kitchen roll
20 cm x 20 cm baking tin
oven gloves
knife

Vegetarian

Dairy Free

INGREDIENTS:

240 g plain white flour (plus an extra teaspoon)
½ teaspoon baking powder
½ teaspoon bicarbonate of soda
¼ teaspoon salt
1 teaspoon cinnamon
1 teaspoon ginger
1 teaspoon allspice
2 large eggs
120 g brown sugar
200 ml honey
1½ teaspoons instant coffee granules
2 tablespoons vegetable oil
4 tablespoons orange juice
40 g raisins
40 g walnuts, chopped
non-stick cooking spray

STEPS:

1 Preheat the oven to 180°C/ Gas mark 4.

2 Soak the raisins in hot water to soften. Leave until you reach step 6.

3 In a medium bowl, combine 240g of flour, baking powder, bicarbonate of soda, salt and the spices.

4 In a large bowl, use the hand mixer, on medium speed, to beat together the eggs, sugar, honey, coffee granules, oil and orange juice.

5 Add half the flour mixture to the wet ingredients. Beat on low until combined. Add the rest of the flour mixture and beat until you have a smooth batter.

6 Drain the raisins and pat dry with kitchen roll. Toss the raisins and nuts in one teaspoon of flour. Fold into the batter.

7 Spray the tin with cooking spray. Pour the batter into the tin. Bake for about 30 minutes.

8 When cooled, cut into 16 squares.

SUKKOT

After Moses led the Israelites out of Egypt (see page 5), they lived for 40 years in temporary shelters, called sukkah, and tents in the desert. Sukkot (the plural of sukkah) is a festival, lasting seven to eight days, to commemorate those years. The first two days of Sukkot are a holiday.

For the festival, Jewish families build their own temporary sukkot to remember their ancestors in the desert. At the end of the festival, there is a celebration of the giving of the law on Sinai, called Simchat Torah.

Now & Then

The sukkah

Traditionally, a sukkah should have a roof of plants, such as bamboo reeds or tree branches. The plant covering must have gaps so that rain can get in and you can see the stars. A sukkah is built so that it is not too comfortable and therefore a reminder of what life is like for the homeless. Decorations include dried vegetables, such as corn, because it is also a celebration of **harvest time**.

A modern sukkah might be put together from a kit. Decorations are sometimes plastic fruits or vegetables. Jews would traditionally eat and sleep in their sukkah, but now they often only share meals there.

Celebrations with plants

During Sukkot, four different types of plants are used in processions, prayers and blessings: branches of palm, myrtle, willow and etrog (a type of citrus fruit). The branches are waved in six different directions to show that God is everywhere, and prayers are said for the rain needed for plants to grow.

Sukkot happens at harvest time in Israel. This means that meals in the sukkah include lots of vegetables and fruit.

⌃ Australian Jews gathering the traditional branches ready for a Sukkot procession.

HANUKKAH

Hanukkah, which is often called the Festival of Lights, is an eight-day holiday in the month of Kislev (see page 7). Hanukkah commemorates an important event in history, when a huge battle was won against foreign enemies. It also commemorates a miracle.

The story of Hanukkah

Over 2,000 years ago, a Syrian king called Antiochus tried to make the Jewish people worship Greek gods instead of following their own faith. The Jewish Temple in Jerusalem was changed into a **pagan** temple. Here, Jews were expected to bow to a statue of Antiochus. A group of Jews, led by Judah of Maccabee, rebelled against Antiochus.

⋁ The menorah is an important part of Hannukah.

The Jews took back their Temple for Jewish worship and prayer. As part of this, they relit the Temple's **menorah** – a seven-branched candlestick with several arms. (Light is a symbol of God's presence and synagogues keep a permanently lit lamp close to the scrolls of the Torah.)

The menorah was fuelled by oil, but they only had enough oil for one day. It would take eight days to make more oil. Miraculously, the one-day supply of oil lasted for eight days. The miracle of the menorah is remembered at Hanukkah by lighting one candle each day.

Now & Then

Menorahs

The Temple's menorah had seven branches, but today's Hanukkah menorahs have nine branches and many use candles, not oil. Eight branches represent each one of the eight miracle days. The last branch is for the candle used to light the other branches, one on each day of Hanukkah.

♥ Families light a seven-branched menorah, in memory of the Temple miracle. A modern-day menorah is known as a chanukiah.

Spinning tops and chocolate money

As well as lighting candles at Hanukkah, Jewish families often play games. One example such a game is dreidel. A dreidel is a four-sided spinning top. On each side of the top is a letter. Together they represent the Hebrew phrase "a great miracle happened there" or, if the game is played in Israel, "a great miracle happened here". This refers to the central Hannukah belief: the miracle of the oil in the Temple.

In Yiddish, the letters are used as commands in the game. For example, after the top has been spun, the side (and the corresponding letter) facing up can tell you to do something. This could be to put in or take out from a central pot of chocolates, raisins or coins.

⋀ The dreidel is a popular way of helping children to remember the great miracle of the oil in the Temple when it was regained by the Jews in around 164 BCE.

Case study

HANUKKAH IN NORTH AMERICA

Hanukkah begins between Thanksgiving (in November) and Christmas. Thanksgiving and Christmas are very popular holidays in the United States and Canada, so for Jews living in these areas, their Hanukkah celebrations can be overshadowed.

To help remind people of Hanukkah, big menorahs are sometimes put up and decorated in parks and other public places in US cities. Musical events for children and parties are organized, too. Because many children are given presents at Christmas, Jewish parents in the United States often give their children presents during Hanukkah, too. In Israel, presents are not exchanged. The only traditional gift in Israel is money, called *gelt*, which is given to children.

⋁ This menorah is in Central Park, New York. The "lighting" of the menorah here is a large public event.

Doughnuts and pancakes

To celebrate the miracle of the oil at Hanukkah, foods cooked or fried in oil are made and eaten. Doughnuts are deep-fried in oil and have jam or other sweet fillings, such as custard or chocolate and cream. Potato pancakes (latkes) are shallow-fried and topped with sweet apple sauce, or a savoury sour cream or cottage cheese. Dairy foods (especially cheesy dishes) are traditionally eaten during Hanukkah, too.

⌃ Many Jewish families have a favourite recipe for latkes, but they are usually based on a mix of potato, egg, onion and flour, or breadcrumbs.

⌃ Israeli shops around the world often display a range of fresh cakes for Hanukkah.

Judith

Another story about bravery of the Jewish people is often told at Hanukkah. The story is about a Jewish widow called Judith and is in a book found outside the main Jewish scriptures, the Apocrypha. The village in which Judith lived was surrounded by Assyrians (see page 45). She went to the Assyrian camp and pretended to surrender to Holofernes, the general of the camp. She gave him lots of salty cheese to make him thirsty so that he drank too much wine. Once he was drunk, she was able to take his sword and kill him. The salty cheese is the reason why cheese and other dairy foods are eaten at Hanukkah.

PURIM

Purim is a holiday that celebrates how Jewish people in **Persia** survived from persecution for over 2,000 years ago because of the bravery of one young woman – Esther. Jews are commanded to have fun at Purim. It's a time for plays, eating and drinking, and happy gatherings at the synagogue.

Story of Esther

In 486 BCE, Xerxes became king of the Persian Empire, where many Jews lived. Xerxes married a woman called Esther, not realizing that she was Jewish. Haman, a powerful nobleman and enemy of the Jews, demanded that Esther's cousin Mordecai bow to him. When Mordecai refused, Haman got permission from Xerxes to kill all the Jewish people. Haman cast lots – as in a lottery – to decide which day the Jews would be killed. "Pur" in "Purim" is a Persian word that means "lot".

⋁ The story of how Esther saved the Jewish people in Persia is in the Book of Esther in the Hebrew Bible.

When Mordecai told Esther Haman's plan, Esther went to ask Xerxes to stop the killing. This was brave because going to see the king without being invited was not allowed, even though she was the king's wife. She could have been executed. But Xerxes loved Esther, so he agreed with her request. Haman was executed and the Jews were saved.

Celebration

One of the Jewish rules says that the scroll of the Book of Esther is read out at Purim. The reading is made into a fun event for families at the synagogues. Children make noises using rattles (called greggars) or by stamping their feet every time the name Haman is read out.

Children also dress up as characters in the Esther story. Before Purim, children often gather to make their own noisemakers and character masks.

⌃ Ready-made Purim greggars of different colours are sold in shops. Children hold the handle, and spin the top round to make a loud noise.

Purim in Israel

Some of the biggest Purim carnivals take place in and around cities in Israel, such as Jerusalem and Tel Aviv. People dress up as characters from the story of Esther. Plays and humorous **parodies** are performed, some even making light-hearted fun of local community leaders.

Tel Aviv holds a Purim street party with top musicians, and there is even a carnival-style Zombie Walk through the streets at night. Here, thousands of local people dress up as zombies to celebrate the survival of the Jewish people when threatened by ancient Persia.

Religious leaders and academics entertain the crowds by writing and performing funny sermons. These are often full of nonsense or fun commentaries on religious writings.

∨ Dressing up is part of the fun for Purim.

Purim baskets

Giving has always been a part of Purim traditions. The Book of Esther requests the "sending of portions from one man to another, and gifts to the poor". In the past, this involved sending a simple gift of two items of food (portions) to at least one person (probably friends or family) and food for the poor.

Today, gifts for family and friends can be simple treats. These could be home-made cakes, or luxurious baskets of food, such as those bought and delivered via a website. Today, money rather than food is often given to the poor, and distributed through charities.

∨ Gifts of food are traditionally sent to one's family or friends in a basket.

Purim feast

Before Purim, some Jews complete a short fast in memory of Esther fasting. She did this before she went to see King Xerxes to ask him to stop Haman from killing the Jews.

For Purim itself, there is a celebratory Purim feast. It usually takes place in the afternoon and many of the foods served are linked to the story of Esther. The most popular Purim food is hamantaschen, a triangular pastry filled with prunes and poppy seeds. There is a recipe for this on pages 28 and 29.

⌃ 'Haman's ears' are among many popular foods for Purim.

Symbolism of hamantaschen

Hamantaschen are triangular in shape to look like a number of things:

• An ear: hamantaschen are sometimes called *oznay Haman* (which means "Haman's ears" in Hebrew). This refers to the tradition of cutting off the ears of people before their execution.

• The purse: Haman wanted to fill with stolen gold from the Jewish people.

• Haman's three-cornered hat.

The three corners might also symbolize Abraham, Isaac and Jacob (the ancestors of the Jewish people). Sometimes, poppy seeds are added to symbolize the bribe money that Haman used to get Xerxes to support his plan to kill all Jews.

There are other symbolic Purim foods. A famous example is challah – a traditional sweet, eggy bread, which is braided to remind people of the rope used to hang Haman. Kreplach are triangular dumplings filled with meat, potato or cabbage. The chopped meat in this traditional food reminds people of how Haman was beaten before he was hanged. The hidden meat may also symbolise other hidden meanings in the story of Esther.

⌄ Challah: sweet braided bread for Purim.

Hamantaschen

Tasty pastries called Hamantaschen are a popular treat for Purim. Traditional fillings include poppy seed, prune and apricot paste.

TIME:

About 2 hours, 15 minutes

SERVES:

Makes 24 pastries

TOOLS:

weighing scales
mixing bowls
regular knife
grater with small holes, or a zester
electric hand whisk
spatula
cling film
rolling pin
8-cm round pastry cutter
baking tray (greased with butter, if not non-stick)
oven gloves
cooling rack

See page 44 for more tips for this recipe!

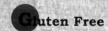 Vegetarian　　Gluten Free

INGREDIENTS:

230 g unsalted butter, softened to room temperature
180 g granulated sugar
1 large egg
½ teaspoon vanilla
1 teaspoon orange zest
280 g plain white flour (plus more for dusting)
1 teaspoon baking powder
¼ teaspoon salt
jam for filling

28

STEPS:

1 Cut the butter into small cubes. In a large bowl, use the hand whisk to beat together the butter and sugar on medium for about one minute until creamy. Add the egg, vanilla and zest, and beat for another minute until combined.

2 In a medium bowl, combine the flour, baking powder and salt. Add half of this flour mixture to the wet ingredients. Whisk on low until combined. Add the rest of the flour mixture, and beat until the dough is stiff.

Scrape the dough out of the bowl and place onto some cling film. Flatten the dough into a disc shape. Wrap and put in the refrigerator for at least an hour.

3

4 Preheat the oven to 180°C/Gas mark 4. Dust a surface and rolling pin with flour. Roll out the dough so it is about 0.3 cm thick. Cut the dough with the pastry cutter, and place the discs on a baking tray, about 2.5 cm apart.

Place a small teaspoonful of filling in the centre of each disc. Fold up three edges, like a triangle, with the centre of filling still exposed. Pinch the corners to seal.

5

6 Bake for 12–14 minutes, or until just browned on the edges. Let cool on the baking sheet for about 2 minutes. Then transfer them to a cooling rack with a clean spatula.

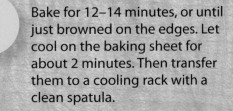

PESACH (PASSOVER)

Pesach (Hebew for Passover) remembers the freeing of the Israelites from slavery (see page 5) and the passing over of the Angel of Death (see below). It is an important eight-day festival and includes a special family meal at the beginning. Strict Jews do not work or go to school during the first two and last two days of Pesach.

Angel of Death

When the Jews were slaves in Egypt, Moses demanded their release. The **pharaoh** refused, so God sent 10 **plagues** to hurt the Egyptian people. These plagues included locusts, frogs and complete darkness.

The tenth plague was the Angel of Death to kill every firstborn in all Egyptian homes. God had told the Jews to mark their doors so that the Angel knew to pass over them. They marked their doors with lambs' blood so that their firstborn were safe.

《Unleavened bread is eaten at Pesach. There are rules about how it should be made. For example, the whole process of mixing and baking should take no more than 18 minutes.

Harvest time

Pesach celebrations also mark the start of a harvest festival on farms in Israel. The following three festivals are known as Pilgrim Festivals in Israel because they are linked to harvesting:

- Pesach marks the time of the barley harvest
- Shavuot takes place when wheat, the last grain crop, is harvested
- Sukkot is the autumn harvest of other field crops and fruit (pages 14–15).

Matzah

Matzah (Hebrew for unleavened) bread is eaten at Pesach to represent the hurry in which the Israelite slaves ran from Egypt. The bread is flat because the slaves did not have time to leave it to rise. It is thefore "unleavened". Leavened bread has yeast in it, to help it rise.

⌃ Barley has been harvested in the Middle East for hundreds of years.

PREPARATIONS FOR PESACH

All over the world, famillies prepare for Pesach with a spring clean. The whole family gets to work on removing all traces of **leaven** and any food that contains leaven. Every room, especially the kitchen, is dusted and washed. Any utensils, such as forks, pots and pans, that have come into contact with leaven are separated and put away. Any food that has leaven in it is given to the poor or put away in a sealed cupboard.

Before going to bed the night before Pesach, children go on a final candlelit search for any leavened bread. Traditionally, adults hide a few pieces for the children to find. When the children discover them, they sweep them into a bag with a feather.

⩔ Jewish children in Russia, on a leaven hunt.

Pesach around the world

Strict Jews around the world do not work or carry out any business transactions on the first two and last two days of Pesach. Children do not go to school on these days either.

But less strict Jews do not follow this. For example, only 10 per cent of Jews in the United States take this time off. Many American Jews prefer to take time off before Pesach to prepare for the big Seder evening meal that marks the start of the festival.

It is a fun time for children, too. For example, some Jewish children re-enact Moses leading the Israelites out of Egypt before Pesach.

⌃ Foods containing leaven are locked away or burnt in preparation for Pesach.

Case study

PESACH IN IRAQ

Jewish children living in Iraq put bags on their backs and re-enact the journey through the desert.

One child asks, "Where are you coming from?"

"From Egypt," replies another child.

"Where are you going?" the third child asks.

"To Jerusalem," the fourth child smiles.

Seder meal

A favourite part of Pesach is the Seder meal, held in the family home or local community at the start of the festival. Seder means "order", and the meal follows a strict order or pattern. It includes blessings, songs, eating matzah and other symbolic foods from a Seder Plate.

Every year in an Orthodox family, the youngest son asks set questions about the meaning of the food and **rituals**. In a Reform household, the youngest son or daughter could ask these questions.

Answers and explanations are read from a book called the Haggadah. This translates as "the telling". The story told is that of the Exodus (the slavery and escape of the Israelites in Egypt, following the arrival of the Angel of Death).

⌃ The main question asked (in Hebrew) at the Seder meal is: why is this night different from all other nights?

The Seder Plate and its symbols are explained below.

- Some foods are dipped in salt water to represent the slaves' tears and the sea that drowned the Egyptians (see page 5).
- Red wine is drunk as a reminder of the blood of the slaves when the Egyptians beat them.
- Four cups of wine are also used to symbolize the four times when God promised freedom to the Israelites, and to symbolize freedom and happiness. Drops from each cup are spilt in sadness as a reminder that the Israelites' freedom cost others their lives.

Bitter herbs – usually horseradish – stand for the bitterness of slavery.

An egg stands for new life, and also Temple **sacrifices**.

Greenery – often lettuce – symbolizes new life.

Haroset – often a paste of apple and spices, such as cinnamon – symbolizes the mortar used between bricks that the slaves had to make in Israel.

A lamb or chicken bone is a reminder of the slaughter of a lamb, the blood of which marked the Israelites' homes so that the Angel of Death would "pass over" them (page 30).

Matzah ball
soup

TIME:

About 2 hours, 15 minutes

SERVES:

up to 4 people

TOOLS:

mixing bowl
weighing scales
whisk
spatula
cling film
large saucepan
plate
knife and cutting board

Dairy Free

At Pesach, Jewish families eat matzah. Unlike other types of bread flour, matzah flour does not rise when baking. It symbolizes the hurry in which the Israelite slaves fled Egypt. If you can't find matzah meal in the store, you can make it by pulsing matzah crackers into a fine dust in a food processor.

See page 44 for more tips on this recipe!

INGREDIENTS:

2 large eggs
2 tablespoons vegetable oil
½ teaspoon salt
⅛ teaspoon pepper
1 teaspoon dried parsley
70 g matzah meal
4 tablespoons fizzy water
750 ml chicken broth
½ of a large onion, diced
2 large carrots, peeled and sliced
2 stalks celery, sliced

STEPS:

1 Whisk the eggs, oil, salt, pepper and parsley together in the bowl.

2 Add the matzah meal and fizzy water. Stir with a spatula until moistened. Don't mix too much.

3 Cover the bowl with cling film and refrigerate for about an hour. The batter will thicken.

4 After about an hour, heat the chicken broth in the large saucepan on the hob. Bring to a boil on high heat.

5 Meanwhile, to make the balls, wet your fingertips and scoop up a tablespoon of batter. Shape it gently into a ball. Set it aside on a plate or surface covered in cling film (see cooking tip on page 44). Repeat with the rest of the batter. Work quickly or the balls will lose their shape.

6 Add the onion, carrots and celery to the boiling broth. Carefully, drop the matzah balls one at a time into the broth. (Let them roll off your fingers away from you to prevent splashing.) When the balls rise to the surface, cover the pot and turn the heat to low.

7 Let the soup simmer, covered, for 30–45 minutes. Try not to open the lid.

8 Ladle two matzah balls into each bowl, and then add the broth.

FAMILY OCCASIONS

Celebrations or rituals can mark rites of passage (different stages in life).

First ceremonies

The first ritual for a boy takes place just after he is born. At eight days old, he is **circumcised** in an event called Brit Milah, which means "covenant of circumcision". This follows a commandment that nearly all Jews follow. Jewish girls are named in the synagogue or at home, and some Jews hold a special naming ceremony 30 days after their birth.

The event also marks how the boy has become part of the covenant between God, Abraham and the Jewish people (see page 5). The baby's Hebrew name is announced at the celebrations. Many Jews are given a second name for day-to-day use, too. Afterwards, there is usually a festive meal.

⩒ A Jewish circumcision ceremony.

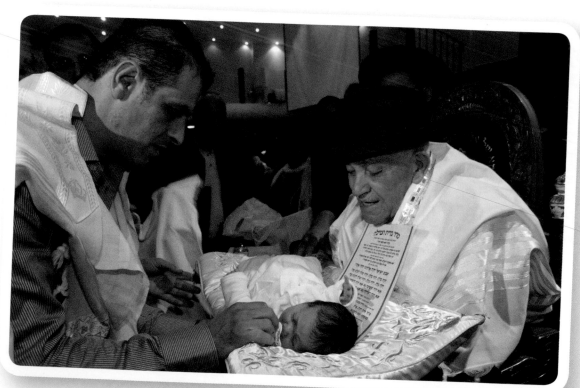

Jewish girls are named in the synagogue on the Shabbat after their birth. Some Jews hold special naming ceremonies for baby girls when they are seven days old.

Coming of age

A person becomes a bar mitzvah (son of the commandment) or a bat mitzvah (daughter of the commandment) when they are traditionally seen as adults. In the past, only boys went through a ceremony for this.

At 13 years old, a boy is seen as a man, and is responsible for following Jewish rules (called mitzvot, the plural of mitzvah) for himself, rather than relying on the guidance of his parents. He will read from the Torah in Hebrew at the synagogue to mark the event. Afterwards, there is a family party.

⌃ Bar – or Bat – Mitzvah usually takes place in a synagogue with family and friends and then can be followed by a party.

Now & Then

Bat Mitzvah

A Jewish girl is traditionally seen as a woman at the age of 12. In the past, it was rare for Jewish families to celebrate their daughter's Bat Mitzvah, but it has become far more common now. There is often a party with family and friends.

Birthdays

There are no Jewish laws about birthdays and it isn't traditional to celebrate them. In fact, it is thought that in the past a birthday was seen as a sad time. This is because a birthday means the person is getting closer to their life's end.

More recently, birthdays are commonly celebrated, just as they are in other cultures. Some synagogues have special services for people when they reach the ages of 70 or 80.

Jewish weddings

Jewish weddings take place under a canopy called a huppah. The huppah symbolizes harmony and the couple's new married home. There are many rituals, for example a ketubah (wedding contract) is read out and blessings are said. Afterwards, the bridegroom breaks a wine glass wrapped in a cloth under his foot to represent the fragile nature of human life. Traditionally, the wedding celebrations go on for a week, with feasts in different people's homes each night.

An Orthodox Jewish wedding in Hungary.

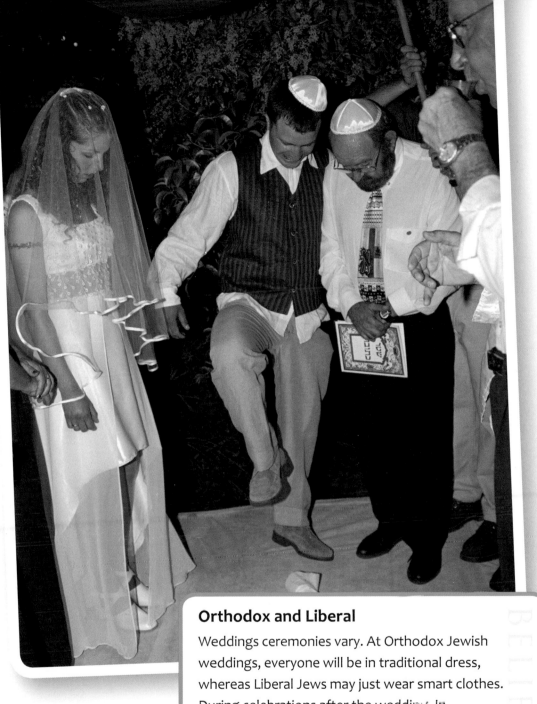

∧ The tradition of the bridegroom breaking the glass happens at both Orthodox and Liberal ceremonies.

Orthodox and Liberal

Weddings ceremonies vary. At Orthodox Jewish weddings, everyone will be in traditional dress, whereas Liberal Jews may just wear smart clothes. During celebrations after the wedding, In Orthodox communities the men and women may separate for any dancing, while others will allow a mixed dance. Orthodox Jews may only have traditional Jewish music, whereas others might choose to have a mix of this and modern songs.

CELEBRATIONS AROUND THE WORLD

Jewish festivals are celebrated all around the world, often following the same customs but with slight differences, depending on the culture of the country. Highlights of many Jewish celebrations are visits to the synagogue, reading holy books such as the Torah, eating special foods and having family gatherings at home.

≪ These Jews in Jerusalem, Israel, are rolling the matzah dough ready for Pesach. Their fur hats are traditionally worn by Hasidic Jews, a branch of Orthodox Judaism.

≫ The Great Synagogue in Pilsen, the Czech Republic – one of the largest synagogues in the world. The Jewish community in the city is now quite small, and only a small area of the synagogue is used for religious services.

In Jewish shops in north London, hamantaschen pastries are on sale for Purim.

A Bar Mitzvah is a time for great celebration, when a boy is seen as responsible for his decisions. These Jews are celebrating near the Wailing Wall in Jerusalem.

This boy is reading the Torah in Hebrew during his Bar Mitzvah ceremony.

COOKERY TIPS

Hamantaschen

- To zest orange or lemon peel, clean the outside of the fruit with water. Use a grater with small holes to take off small bits of the fragrant outer peel. Don't grate too deep – the white part is bitter.

- Spread some flour on your work surface and rolling pin to keep the dough from sticking.

Honey cake

- Dried spices can lose their smell and flavour if kept too long. The best place to store them is in a kitchen cupboard away from the heat of the stove. Spices stay freshest in dry, cool places out of sunlight.

- Non-stick cooking spray is an easy way to keep your food from sticking to a baking pan. If you don't have non-stick spray, you can simply rub some vegetable oil on the pan with a paper towel.

Matzah ball soup

- You will need to use a whisk in this recipe. Unlike stirring, the quick action of whisking introduces air into a mixture, which helps to make it light and fluffy.

- Place your matzah balls on cling film, not a floured surface. They might pick up some of the flour, which can change their consistency. Also, regular flour contains yeast and leaven, and these balls are supposed to be unleavened.

TIMELINE

BCE

c. 1300–1200	The Exodus of Israelites from slavery in Egypt under Moses, which is celebrated at Pesach. The people's wandering in tents in the desert for the next 40 years is marked at Sukkot and the giving of the Torah at Simchat Torah
587	Babylonian Exile begins after conquest by the Assyrians; this event is linked to the story of Judith told at Hanukkah
486–465	Reign of Persian King Xerxes I: the heroism of his Jewish wife, Esther, is marked at the festival of Purim
175	King Antiochus Epiphanes comes to the throne: later, he places a statue in the Jerusalem Temple to be worshipped
164	Capture and re-dedication of the Jerusalem Temple by the Maccabees, which is celebrated at Hanukkah

CE

70	The Romans destroy the Jerusalem Temple
135	The Romans force out Jews from the whole country of Judea
1933–1945	Nazi oppression of Jews resulting in HaShoah, the death of 6 million Jews. It is marked on Yom HaShoah (27 Nisan) and is also known as Holocaust Memorial Day.
1948	Establishment of the State of Israel as a homeland for the Jewish people; it is marked by an Independence Day In April

GLOSSARY

challah (hallah) sweet, eggy bread that is often braided and eaten on Shabbat (Sabbath) and at celebrations such as Rosh Hashanah

circumcised foreskin of the penis has been removed

covenant promise, or agreement, in Judaism between God and Abraham, and his descendants (the Jewish people)

fast go without food or drink for a particular period of time

harvest time when crops have been gathered in and the crops are celebrated

Hebrew early name given to the Jewish people; the language in which the Torah and other Jewish scriptures are written and recited; also the traditional language of many Jews

Hebrew Bible sacred Jewish writings, also called the Old Testament or Tanakh

Holocaust deliberate killing of 6 million Jews and others by Nazi Germany and its supporters during World War II

Israelites name given to the Jewish people after they were known as Hebrews, but before they were called Jews

Jewish Law (also called Halakhah) beliefs of the Jewish people, and also the rules and practices affecting everyday life, ranging from food to celebration customs

leaven yeast or another raising agent that makes dough or batter rise

matzah flat bread without leaven, especially important at Passover (Pesach)

menorah candle-holder with nine branches, or the seven-branched candle-holder in the Temple

pagan people or a place linked to the worship of many gods, such as in classical Rome

parody take-off, in which people imitate something or someone in a humorous way

Persia area covering southwest Asia, which is now Iran

pharaoh name for the ruler in Ancient Egypt

plague disease that spreads quickly and can kill many people

repentance feeling sorry or shameful about something one has done, or should have done, and seeking forgiveness from God

ritual religious ceremony or custom

sacrifice offering made to God

Shabbat (Sabbath) day of rest, once a week, when Jewish people usually go to the synagogue

slave person who works for no money and has little freedom to do as he or she wishes

synagogue Jewish place of worship

Torah first five books of the Hebrew Bible

World War II global war lasting from 1939 to 1945

Find out more

Books
Anne Frank: The Authorized Graphic Biography, Sid Jacobson (Macmillan's Children's Books, 2015)
Jewish Holidays Cookbook (Dorling Kindersley, 2008)
The Diary of Young Girl, Anne Frank (Penguin, 2012)

Websites
www.akhlah.com
Learn all you need to know about Judaism on the website of the Jewish Children's Learning Network.

www.bbc.co.uk/schools/religion/judaism/index.shtml
Learn more about Judaism and its festivals on the BBC website.

www.chabad.org/calendar/view/month.htm
Use this website to find the dates of Jewish celebrations on the Gregorian calendar.

Places to visit
Jewish Museum London
Raymond Burton House
129–131 Albert Street
London NW1 7NB
www.jewishmuseum.org.uk
See collections on the history of the Jewish community in Britain in this museum.

You could also contact your local synagogue to arrange a visit. It is a good idea to contact them in advance to arrange to visit. You should always be quiet and respectful in any place of worship.

Further research
Find more celebration foods to cook and taste, such as for Pesach:
www.bbc.co.uk/food/occasions/passover

INDEX